ideals® CHRISTMAS

70TH ANNIVERSARY EDITION

A special anniversary
collection, including new material
and classics from the past

*"As the name implies—a book of old-fashioned
Christmas ideals, homey philosophy,
poetry, music, inspiration, and art."*

—THE DESCRIPTION FROM THE FIRST ISSUE
OF *IDEALS*, PUBLISHED IN 1944

IDEALS PUBLICATIONS

NASHVILLE, TENNESSEE

ISBN-13: 978-0-8249-1346-5

Published by Ideals Publications
A Guideposts Company
Nashville, Tennessee
www.idealsbooks.com

Printed and bound in the U.S.A.
Printed on Weyerhaeser Lynx. The paper used in this publication meets the mini-
mum requirements of American National Standard for Information Sciences—
Permanence of Paper for Printed Materials, ANSI Z39.48-1984.

Publisher, Peggy Schaefer
Editor, Melinda L. R. Rumbaugh
Copy Editors, Debra Wright and Rachel Pate
Designer, Marisa Jackson
Permissions Editor, Kristi West

Cover: CHRISTMAS TREE HILL by Bonnie White. Image © Bonnie White/Next Day
Art
Inside front cover: Painting by Frans Van Lamsweerde. Image © Ideals Publications
Inside back cover: Painting by Frans Van Lamsweerde. Image © Ideals Publications
Page 3: Photograph © Jumping Rocks Photography/Gap Interior Images Ltd.

Sheet Music for "I Heard the Bells on Christmas Day" by Dick Torrans, Melode,
Inc. Additional art credits: Pages 8–9, 26–27, 50, and back cover art by Kathy
Rusynyk. The following pages contain art © [the artist]/Shutterstock.com: 4,
anemad; 8, effrosyni; 11, kaadesigns, Sundra, Nataliia Litovchenko; 12,
Moljavka; 14–15, anfisa focusova; 16–17, Astromonkey, homydesign; 19, Pim;
24, Shapovalova Elena, elxeneize; 28, Togataki, lozas; 30, Sundra; 33, privilege,
100ker; 34 and 64, arigato; 36–37, Alena P; 39, 40, and 43, Flas100, Turkan Akyol,
Henry Hazboun; 46 and 60, Supertrooper; 46, Fernando Cortes; 57,
Elena Kalistratova.

ACKNOWLEDGMENTS
WILSON, RALPH F. "The Cradle, A Christmas Story" Copyright © Ralph F. Wilson,
pastor@joyfulheart.com. All rights reserved. Used by permission.
    Our Thanks to the following authors or their heirs: Dana K. Akers, Edith Shaw
Butler, Louise Pugh Corder, Joan Donaldson, Mark Edwards, Dorothy Elam, Lisa A.
Goff, Keith H. Graham, Frances Minturn Howard, Edna Jaques, Pamela Kennedy,
Ruth Kephart, Brian F. King, Pamela Love, Douglas Malloch, A. K. Rowswell, Garnett
Ann Schultz, Helen Whiteman Shick, Diane Skinner, Laurence Smith, Eileen Spinelli,
Grace Mathews Walker, Mary Stoner Wine.
    Scripture quotations, unless otherwise indicated, are taken from King James
Version (KJV). Scripture quotations marked NIV are taken from the HOLY BIBLE, NEW
INTERNATIONAL VERSION®. Copyright © 1973, 1978, 1984 Biblica. Used by per-
mission of Zondervan. All rights reserved.
    Every effort has been made to establish ownership and use of each selection in this
book. If contacted, the publisher will be pleased to rectify any inadvertent errors or
omissions in subsequent editions.

Join the community of Ideals readers on Facebook at:
www.facebook.com/IdealsMagazine
Readers are invited to submit original poetry and prose for possible use in future
publications. Please send no more than four typed submissions to: Magazine
Submissions, Ideals Publications, 2630 Elm Hill Pike, Suite 100, Nashville,
Tennessee 37214. Manuscripts will be returned if a self-addressed stamped
envelope is included.

The Birchwood Inn

Now comes the time when love holds sway,
and grown-ups share in children's play,
and houses glow with varied light
and make a fairy-time of night,
and life is rich and warm and full,
and heartstrings feel the tender pull.
—MARK EDWARDS

*May the wonder of the season
fill your heart with love and joy;
may you know the
world's first Christmas
started with a little Boy.*
—JUNE MASTERS BACHER

Christmas Gifts

Dorothy L. Elam

I'm grateful for the Christmas gifts
God freely gave to me—
the gift of love, the gift of hope,
faith, and charity.

These were the things I needed most
when I felt that no one cared;
then I discovered this was a doubt
that many others shared.

So I decided to give to them
some of God's gifts to me
and found the more I gave away,
the more came back to me.

Now I thank Thee, Babe of Bethlehem,
for the gifts You gave to me
that never fade nor tarnish,
good for eternity.

Because

Mary Stoner Wine

I saw the candlelight's soft glow,
a gleaming path across the snow,
and through the window's filmy lace,
there came a radiant, subtle grace;
for Christmas trees with burning light,
adorned to greet the holy night,
from every window, each hearthstone,
with hope's expectant gladness shone.
Oh, homes so beautiful, so bright,
reflecting joy and peace and light;
oh, homes that send through winter's chill
your silent hymn of peace, good will—
why do your cozy hearth fires burn
and those you sheltered now return?
Because, to you, from heaven above
there came God's gift—God's gift of love.

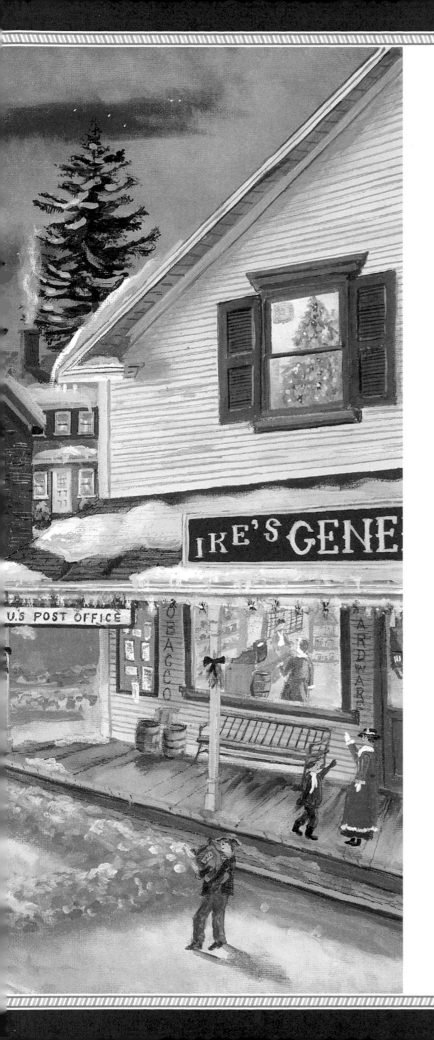

The Road to Christmas

Garnett Ann Schultz

On the pleasant road to Christmas,
round a bend that leads to home,
there is laughter in the snowflakes
such as none you've ever known.
You can see a lighted window
ever bright and ever fair,
and the sounds of Christmas music
fill the crisp, cold winter air.
Happy faces there to greet you
when at last the day is done,
with a welcome on the doorstep
reaching out to everyone.
Lots of mistletoe and holly,
little ones who still believe,
'cause they know that dear old Santa
will be there on Christmas Eve.
You will find the road to Christmas
where your hopes and dreams come true,
and your heart will know the magic
that the season brings to you.
All the world's a little brighter
at this special time of year—
peace on earth, because it's Christmas,
bits of gladness, smiles of cheer.
May you know a joy this Christmas
that will fill your heart with love;
may your music be the music
of the angels up above.
With the home-fires softly glowing
may you find my wish sincere,
as the pleasant road to Christmas
leads you through a bright new year.

IKE'S GENERAL STORE by Bob Fair.
Image © Bob Fair/Next Day Art

Bits & Pieces

Be merry all, be merry all,
with holly dress the festive hall;
prepare the song, the feast, the ball,
to welcome merry Christmas all.
—*W. R. Spencer*

December, month of holly, pine, and balsam,
of berries red, of candles' mellow light,
of home and fireside, laughter, happy faces,
of peace that comes upon the holy night.
—*Author Unknown*

Deck the halls with boughs of holly,
fa la la la la, la la la la!
'Tis the season to be jolly,
fa la la la la, la la la la!
—*Thomas Oliphant*

Villagers all, this frosty tide,
let your doors swing open wide;
though wind may follow and snow betide,
yet draw us in by your fire to bide:
joy shall be yours in the morning.
—*Kenneth Grahame*

Heap on more wood!—
the wind is chill;
but let it whistle as it will,
we'll keep our Christmas merry still.
—*Sir Walter Scott*

*Glad Christmas comes, and every hearth
makes room to give him welcome now.
—John Clare*

*Sing hey! Sing hey!
for Christmas Day;
twine mistletoe and holly,
for friendship glows
in winter snows,
and so let's all be jolly.
—Author Unknown*

*So now is come our joyful feast;
let every man be jolly;
each room with ivy leaves is dressed
and every post with holly.
And whilst we thus inspired sing,
let all the streets with echoes ring;
woods and hills and everything
bear witness we are merry.
—George Wither*

The Spell of Silver Bells

Helen Whiteman Shick

Under the spell of silver bells,
old pleasures of long ago
come seeping out of memory's well
to brighten the Christmas glow.

The tinkly, silvery echo-chimes
are melodies out of the past,
for they sing of childhood's happy times
—the wonderful joys that will last.

Under the spell of silver bells,
there's a tree all spangled and bright,
and carols the holiday joys foretell,
making laughter on Christmas night.

A great holly wreath at the window hangs,
and stockings are bulging too;
there's a heavenly scent of evergreen tang
and a firelight sparkling anew.

A big paper bell from the chandelier
is hanging with mistletoe near it;
and candles are flickering mellowness
for a room full of Christmas spirit.

There's a home where a family
of loved ones dwell
in the picture of long, long ago,
as memory quickens with silver bells
to brighten the Christmas glow.

Christmas Tree
Laurence Smith

Star over all,   green under tinsel,
eye of the night,   glitter and glow,
stand on my tree,   appled with baubles,
magical sight,   silver and gold,
green under frost,   spangled with fire,
green under snow,   warm over cold.

Hodgepodge Tree
Louise Pugh Corder

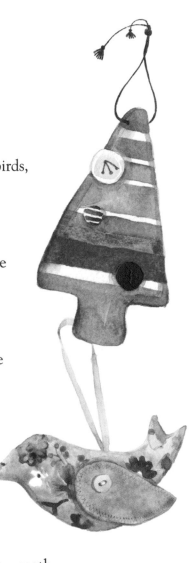

Designer trees are beautiful,
a wonder to behold—
all draped in garlands, crimson birds,
in silver bells or gold.
But I'm a sentimental soul
who thrives on memory.
Each ornament is hung with love
upon my hodgepodge tree.
The crooked star upon the top
is one my daughter made
of beads she strung on floral wire
when she was in third grade.

The toothpick snowflakes,
    painted cones
are treasures dear to me.
My youngest son
    helped fashion them,
and he was only three.
A clothespin angel, bread-dough wreath,
imperfect handmade art—
each thing recalls a Christmas past
that's special to my heart.

Photograph © Nick Carter/GAP Interior Images Ltd.

Merry Christmas
Author Unknown

In the rush of the merry morning,
when the red burns through the gray
and the wintry world lies waiting
for the glory of the day,
then we hear a fitful rushing
just without upon the stair,
see two white phantoms coming,
catch the gleam of sunny hair.

Are they Christmas fairies stealing
rows of little socks to fill?
Are they angels floating hither
with their message of good will?
What sweet spell are these
   elves weaving,
as like larks they chirp and sing?
Are these palms of peace from heaven
that these lovely spirits bring?

Rosy feet upon the threshold,
eager faces peeping through,
with the first red ray of sunshine,
chanting cherubs come in view;
mistletoe and gleaming holly,
symbols of a blessed day,
in their chubby hands they carry,
streaming all along the way.

Well we know them, never weary
of this innocent surprise;
waiting, watching, listening always
with full hearts and tender eyes,
while our little household angels,
white and golden in the sun,
greet us with the sweet
   old welcome—
"Merry Christmas, every one!"

Christmas Memories of an Old Dime Store

Lisa A. Goff

As I helped package 600 pounds of holiday chocolates for a friend at his old variety store recently, the intoxicating scent transported me back to Christmastimes in the 1960s when, as a child, I would go into another old dime store. The screen door would squeak as I pulled it open, the thumb latch clicked as I pressed it and pushed open the heavy wood and glass door, and the scent of chocolates and hot cashews whooshed out.

The old wooden floor creaked as I moved across it, heading straight to the candy counter. Cashews and peanuts were always under the heat lamp inside the glass case, but during the holiday season, loose, unwrapped chocolates in bushel baskets were lined up on the floor around the counter.

No matter how tempted I was by the smell of chocolates, I always spent my coins on the delicious, warm cashews, eagerly watching the clerk lift an aluminum scoopful of the golden morsels and slide them into a white paper bag. Then I popped a handful in my mouth and, while looking around at all the fascinating store goods, ate as many as I could while they were still warm. They were best that way—warm. If they cooled or I couldn't finish them, I would twist the top of my bag shut and take the rest home to Grandpa. He loved cashews hot or not.

Each December, when we were really small, usually on a blustery Saturday afternoon, Grandma would take me and my sister to the dime store to do our Christmas shopping, giving us each the same budgeted amount of money (a dollar maximum for each family member on the shopping lists that we had tediously written sometime after Thanksgiving).

I picked the prettiest embroidered lace hankies for the ladies—the grandmas, my aunts, and Mom. For the men, it was usually Old Spice cologne or cigars for Grandpa, squeeze-open coin purses or plaid hankies for the uncles and Grandad. For Aunt Rosealice it was a dollar box of her favorite chocolate-covered cherry cordials. For my sister I picked something that I would like to have myself, such as paper dolls, a paddle-ball, coloring books, or a colorful cardboard kaleidoscope.

Back at home, Grandma took the centerpiece off the kitchen table and brought in bags of wrapping paper and ribbons. We proudly dumped our precious gifts onto the table, showing each other what we had purchased for whom. We always started out hiding what we got for each other, but by the time we finished wrapping gifts, we would have whispered the secret in each other's ears and sometimes conspired to switch and keep the gifts for ourselves.

The gift wrapping always took up the rest of the afternoon, and Grandma would sit in the front room and read or nap in her chair. She

sometimes started cooking supper before we were finished, and soon the kitchen was filled with the oven's warmth and steam from boiling potatoes.

The steam would cover the windows as the sun began to set, and before long the windows would be black from the darkness outside. I always hated and feared the darkness outside those windows, but loved the smells of Grandma's cooking and the warmth and coziness inside.

With the wrapping finished, our mess cleared, and the table set, I was tired and full of nuts and chocolates and giddily anticipating how happy my beloved family members would be when they opened my gifts to them. I was filled with pride and happiness for the day's accomplishments. I

was replete with a day's worth of memories that would last a lifetime.

Now, I often think how my little bits of giving must have been humorous to them all and how every year they acted so surprised and grateful for my "generous" gifts purchased with my grandparents' money.

It didn't matter to them that they got a hankie every year. Though presents for me were piled under the tree, the most wonderful gifts to me were their feigned surprise and happy praises of "ooh and ah" while holding up their gifts for all to see. Aunt Rosealice always shared her cordials with me. Those were gifts of love that they gave me.

Christmas Sled
Author Unknown

Oh, for the winters that used to be—
the winters that only a boy may see!
Rich with the snowflakes' rush and swirl;
keen as a diamond, pure as a pearl;
brimming with healthful, rollicking fun;
sweet with their rest when the play
    was done,
with kindly revels each day decreed,
and a Christmas sled for the royal steed.

Down from the crest with shrill hurray!
Clear the track, there! Out of the way!
Scarcely touching the path beneath,
scarce admitting of breath to breathe,
dashing along, with leap and swerve,
over the crossing, round the curve.
Talk of your flying machines! Instead,
give me the swoop of that Christmas sled.

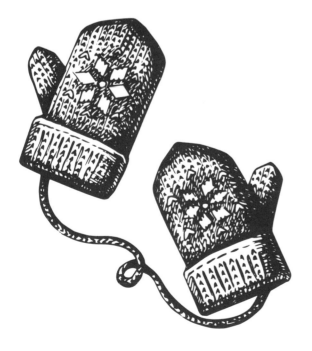

Memories in Fresh-Fallen Snow
Keith H. Graham

A sleepy man with silver-gray hair
peered through a window by his rocking chair.
He looked back to good times lived long ago,
when laughing children, with faces aglow,
created memories in fresh-fallen snow.

Boys and girls would gather for daylong play
on a neighborhood lawn on a snowy day.
They'd build snowmen with skill and might,
packing and sculpting to make them just right;
then use them as shields in a snowball fight.

He recalled the blizzard forty years ago
that buried his world under two feet of snow.
When the winds ceased and the skies
    turned blue,
adventurous children found much to do,
like making caves in drifts all the days through.

Once, for five nights before Christmas Day,
he played a lone shepherd in a manger display.
While his angel sisters flaunted their wings
and Mom, as Mary, led in carols to sing,
worshipers admired the baby doll King.

"Wake up, Grandpa," a little boy said.
"Today's Christmas! It's snowing!
    I have a new sled!"
The man rocked to his feet when he heard,
    "Let's go!"
Then laughing and singing, with faces aglow,
they carved new memories in fresh-fallen snow.

Portrait of Winter

Brian F. King

Now, blissfully, the woodlands dream
where winter crowns each sleeping hill;
where silent shadows blend and twine
in drowsy valleys, white and still.

Now, tinkling brooklets softly sing
sweet slumber songs to snows that lie
where seedlings dream of spring to come
beneath a bleak December sky.

Contentment dwells where nature's hand
has sketched a winter wonderland.

~

Announced by all the trumpets of the sky,
arrives the snow, and, driving o'er the fields,
seems nowhere to alight: the whited air
hides hills and woods, the river, and the heaven,
and veils the farmhouse at the garden's end.
The sled and traveler stopped, the courier's feet
delayed, all friends shut out, the housemates sit
around the radiant fireplace, enclosed
in a tumultuous privacy of storm.
—RALPH WALDO EMERSON

Through My Window

That's Brilliant!

Pamela Kennedy

When our kids were young, one of our daughter's favorite Christmas Eve traditions was taking a drive to look at Christmas lights. She'd sit patiently during the Christmas Eve service, and at the end, hold her small white candle very still through all the verses of "Silent Night." Then, as we left the church, she'd turn her shining eyes upward and ask in a dramatic whisper, "Now, Mama?" For her, driving past homes and businesses decked out in sparkling holiday lights was the brilliant "Amen" to the wonder of the Christmas story.

She's a grown-up married lady now, but this past December, when she and her husband visited from Chicago, we decided to revive the old custom. I did some pre-Christmas reconnoitering and discovered there were two displays in our neighborhood that had garnered statewide attention and were must-sees.

The first was at the home of a local jeweler. We spotted the sparkling star atop his house a few blocks away and followed it and the trail of cars inching along toward its incandescent glow like latter-day magi. When we arrived, someone jokingly remarked that it looked like the jeweler had brought his work home! Over 350,000 lights glistened from his roof, outlined every tree branch, edged every window, and blazed from his front

yard. As we strolled the sidewalk in front of the house, I kept trying to figure out the theme: There were polar bears, geese, and a small herd of deer bobbing their lighted antlers. A merry-go-round spun in circles next to an electric train traversing a miniature alpine landscape. Mary, Joseph, and Baby Jesus glowed serenely in a wooden stall flanked by a life-sized eight-point buck and a couple of angels. Above their heads, the regular contingent of reindeer plus Rudolph towed Santa's sleigh, followed closely by Snoopy, Winnie the Pooh, and a host of Disney characters. Lighted candy canes, carolers, lollipops, an extended family of snowmen, snowflakes, angels, assorted holiday inflatables, and stars all jostled with myriad strings of lights and icicles. A prominently placed sign declared: "Wise Men Still Seek Him"—which, in this case, I considered both literally and figuratively true! This was a Christmas light display that would make the Griswold family (of National Lampoon's *Christmas Vacation* fame) look stingy. Just when I thought I had seen everything, something else peeked out at me from behind a shrub or up in a tree.

But this was just the first stop. If the jeweler's display was over the top in quantity, the next display, a "Christmas Spectacular," beat it out in quality. Created from over 600 strings of LED lights, 5,000 feet of extension cords, and 7,000 zip

ties (according to their website), this Christmas light show included synchronized animation and illumination all choreographed to music by a sophisticated computer program called "Light O Rama." It was bigger, brassier, and definitely more boisterous! When the first set started, the entire front yard pulsed to a techno version of "Amazing Grace." The beat went on as the US Navy Band launched into their rendition of "Dueling Jingle Bells" while streamers of LED lights throbbed in time to the music and half a dozen Christmas trees flashed in syncopation. Hoops of light leapt across the yard and back, all under the undulating beacon of a twelve-foot star. Just watching the display was exhausting! Things finally mellowed out a bit as Elvis crooned "Blue Christmas" while thousands of cerulean lights shimmered in time to the music. We didn't even notice the chilly drizzle as we stood across the street—heads tilted back, mouths agape—while each successive production

number outdid the one before. Children danced on the walkways, bouncing in time to the music and shrieking every time Charlie, the animated snowman, announced the next selection. Finally, when the Trans Siberian Orchestra hit the last chord of "Wizards in Winter," after twenty-five minutes of non-stop lights and music, I was ready for a long winter nap! I turned to ask "What's happened to Christmas?" but then looked at my grown daughter's face, shining in the reflection of those tens of thousands of Christmas lights, and saw once more the little girl from so many years ago, eyes aglow from the light of her single white Christmas Eve candle. And that's when I got it. The lights of the holiday season might take different shapes, colors, and even sounds for each generation, but the true Light remains the same—still bringing joy and wonder to people of all ages—and that's the brilliance of Christmas!

Christmas Lights and the Light

Keith H. Graham

I sit alone in a darkened room facing a Christmas tree. It appears to be nothing more than a black silhouette.

Relaxing, smiling, I flip a switch. Instantly, darkness vanishes, and a quiet explosion of beauty overwhelms the place. Multi-colored rainbows send their streamers in all directions, across branches and into the darkest corners. Ornaments, once invisible, now convert their sparkles into reflections across every wall and upon my eyes. The ceiling becomes an evening sky displaying galaxies of tiny, twinkling stars.

Once again, I realize how much I like Christmas lights. They dispel darkness and create beauty.

Comfortable, I close my eyes and think about what happened in Bethlehem two millennia ago. Under the cover of darkness, in a dimly lit stable, upon a golden mound of hay, God placed His Son.

Common shepherds—stationed on the hillside fields, performing their humble and necessary duties—were the first to hear the birth announcement. While bathed in the light of God's glory, they heard the good news spoken by an angel. Later, stately Wise Men would be guided to the scene by the brilliance of a special star.

A song of joy now stirs in my heart because I know that the Baby laid in the manger was much more than an earthly newborn. He was Jesus, the Savior; He was Immanuel, His Father's very presence. He was the Light of the world Who could and would conquer the deepest, darkest corners of sin by the continuous, all-sufficient brilliance of His truth.

Again and again, whether at Christmastime or any given day of the year, I realize how much I love the Light. He dismisses darkness and creates the most perfect beauty.

Photograph © Costas Picadas/
GAP Interior Images Ltd.

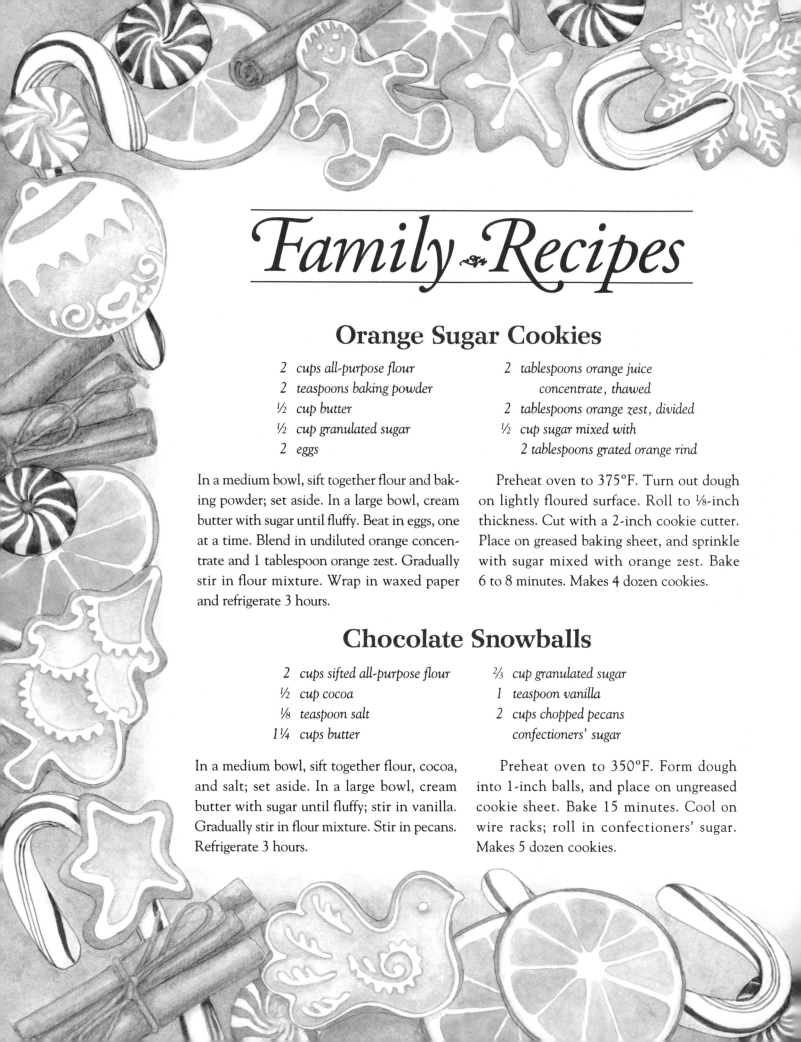

Family ❦ Recipes

Orange Sugar Cookies

2 cups all-purpose flour
2 teaspoons baking powder
½ cup butter
½ cup granulated sugar
2 eggs

2 tablespoons orange juice
  concentrate, thawed
2 tablespoons orange zest, divided
½ cup sugar mixed with
  2 tablespoons grated orange rind

In a medium bowl, sift together flour and baking powder; set aside. In a large bowl, cream butter with sugar until fluffy. Beat in eggs, one at a time. Blend in undiluted orange concentrate and 1 tablespoon orange zest. Gradually stir in flour mixture. Wrap in waxed paper and refrigerate 3 hours.

Preheat oven to 375°F. Turn out dough on lightly floured surface. Roll to ⅛-inch thickness. Cut with a 2-inch cookie cutter. Place on greased baking sheet, and sprinkle with sugar mixed with orange zest. Bake 6 to 8 minutes. Makes 4 dozen cookies.

Chocolate Snowballs

2 cups sifted all-purpose flour
½ cup cocoa
⅛ teaspoon salt
1¼ cups butter

⅔ cup granulated sugar
1 teaspoon vanilla
2 cups chopped pecans
  confectioners' sugar

In a medium bowl, sift together flour, cocoa, and salt; set aside. In a large bowl, cream butter with sugar until fluffy; stir in vanilla. Gradually stir in flour mixture. Stir in pecans. Refrigerate 3 hours.

Preheat oven to 350°F. Form dough into 1-inch balls, and place on ungreased cookie sheet. Bake 15 minutes. Cool on wire racks; roll in confectioners' sugar. Makes 5 dozen cookies.

Gingerbread Cookies

3½ cups all-purpose flour	½ cup butter, softened
1 teaspoon baking soda	¾ cup granulated sugar
1 teaspoon ground cinnamon	1 egg
1 teaspoon ground ginger	¼ cup dark molasses
½ teaspoon salt	3 tablespoons orange juice

In a medium bowl, sift together flour, baking soda, cinnamon, ginger, and salt; set aside. In a large bowl, cream butter with sugar until fluffy. Add egg, molasses, and orange juice; beat well. Gradually stir in flour mixture. Divide dough in half and wrap in plastic wrap. Chill 1 hour or until firm enough to handle.

Preheat oven to 350°F. On a greased baking sheet, roll out half of dough to ⅛-inch thickness. Cut out desired shapes and remove excess dough from baking sheet with a spatula. Bake 10 minutes. Cool on baking sheet 1 minute; transfer to wire racks to cool. Makes about 3 dozen cookies.

White-Chocolate Candy-Cane Cookies

1 cup granulated sugar	½ cup butter, softened
1 teaspoon baking powder	2 eggs
½ teaspoon salt	1 teaspoon vanilla
8 ounces white chocolate baking squares, divided	2¾ cups all-purpose flour
	⅔ cup finely crushed candy canes

Preheat oven to 350°F. In a small bowl, combine sugar, baking powder, and salt; set aside. Chop 4 ounces white chocolate; set aside. In a small saucepan, melt remaining 4 ounces white chocolate over low heat; remove from heat and cool slightly. In a large bowl, cream butter until fluffy. Beat in eggs and vanilla. Add sugar mixture; beat until combined. Stir in melted white chocolate. Gradually stir in flour mixture. Fold in chopped white chocolate and crushed candy canes. Drop by rounded teaspoons 2 inches apart onto a parchment-paper-lined cookie sheet. Bake 12 to 15 minutes or until cookies are lightly browned around edges. Cool on baking sheet 1 minute; transfer to wire racks to cool. Makes 3 to 4 dozen cookies.

Christmas Cookie Magic
Louise Pugh Corder

There is in childhood's treasure chest
a custom I remember best—
the special, yearly family treat
when we baked Christmas cookies sweet.
An expert cook, Mom cast her spell.
Her students creamed and sifted well.
The room became a magic place;
we watched Mom mix and knead with grace.
Then every child, bright eyes aglow,
rolled out a precious bit of dough
and cut out well-chosen shapes with care
in spicy, fragrant Christmas air.
As cookies into oven went,
our mouths all watered at the scent—
till out they came, a welcome sight,
quite golden brown and baked just right.
Each one of us would sample one
the very minute they were done
and frost the Santa, Christmas tree,
bell, star, and reindeer shapes with glee.
In modern kitchen I recall
our cookie fun when I was small,
get out Mom's favorite recipes,
and plan to make some memories.

Photograph © Studio Barcelona/Shutterstock

Christmas

Frances Minturn Howard

If the green trees of winter
moved indoors to houses,
the hemlocks, the cedars,
the spruces, the pines,
cold in their forests
moved in by the fire,
their thick juices warmed
into pungent sweet scent—
it would smell, yes,
   it would smell
like Christmas.

If all of the sounds
were there for our hearing—
the rustle of tissue,
the clinking of glass,

the small chiming sound
of the ornaments brushing
one on another,
the ringing of bells—
it would sound, yes,
   it would sound
like Christmas.

If globes of thin gold
dangled before us,
fragile and brilliant
as fruit of our dreams;
if candles were lighted
nimbused and flaming,
touching with splendor
the fruit and the tree—

it would look, yes,
   it would look
like Christmas.

But it would not be
   Christmas—
no, never, not Christmas—
unless there were something
abroad in the air,
warmer than snow and
lighter than raindrops,
a softness, a wonder
that Christmas brings here,
a rebirth, a promise
large on the air.

Christmas Chest

Joan Donaldson

When the snowstorms of January swirl outside our windows, I pack away our crèche and ponder what I should make for next year's Christmas presents. I will need a full year to complete the many projects that I will hide from my family in my grandmother's cedar chest.

After my grandparents passed away, my mother and aunts gathered in their small home, tucked back from a narrow road lined with maples. As a child and into adulthood, I loved visiting my grandparents' small farm flanked by vineyards, asparagus fields, and pastures. My cousins and I roamed the countryside, stopping to play on the swings at the nearby one-room schoolhouse. Our parents knew we were safe. Having left behind my town life, I reveled in the rural freedom. If the weather was rainy or too hot, we kids played in my grandparents' basement; often three or four of us perched on the cedar chest, looking at my grandmother's albums of vintage postcards. Or when I had to wait for my cousins to arrive, I would flop on it and read.

So when the three daughters divided up their parents' furniture, they asked each grandchild which two pieces he or she would like to inherit. I requested the chest, and my cousins agreed that I should have it because I loved to knit, and at that time I was spinning fleece into yarn. I had remembered a moment when my grandmother and I knelt by the chest, opening it to remove a wool blanket. The woodsy scent of cedar had drifted across the room, and she had explained that the cedar fragrance kept moths away from woolen articles. Many years later, my husband loaded the trunk into his pickup, and later that day we positioned it in our bedroom. I rubbed the lid with lemon oil, while remembering my grandmother.

Throughout the year—as I knitted wool mittens, socks, or sweaters—I would pop them into the chest, squirreling away my Christmas gifts. One day, I realized that instead of hiding other purchased presents in various out-of-the-way cupboards, where I sometimes forgot about them, I should slip them into the chest. So I nestled books, CDs, puzzles, or other small items between the mittens and socks.

Now, when Advent arrives, I open the chest, inhaling the spicy scent, and remove some of the gifts. While wrapping them, I recall the mound of presents beneath my grandparents' Christmas tree and how my cousins and I would sit on the floor, guessing what was hidden beneath the wrapping paper. Slowly, my packages covered in red paper with holly leaves or scattered with white snowflakes fill baskets in a corner of our guest bedroom. I anticipate each person's delight as the presents are opened, while remembering my own pleasure in sewing quilts or knitting lace doilies. All too soon, Christmas Day arrives with a flurry of excitement and activities, but the joy of the season flows throughout the year as I create and hide new gifts in my grandmother's cedar chest.

The Search

Diane Skinner

Searching for the Christ Child was a grueling task for three Wise Men, but they never gave up. When I was issued a similar challenge from our pastor to look for signs of a Christ Child during Advent, I was ready.

It was Monday, and my day was packed with activities, including some Christmas shopping at the mall. I was greeted by flashing lights, a Santa house, and a bellowing choo-choo train. Every window was decorated with sale signs and ornaments.

Strolling past stores, I was dazzled by holiday decorations, but I did not hear a Christmas carol or see evidence of the Christ Child. I loved the colored lights, but it saddened me that Christ was not included in the glitz. I pondered how stores could celebrate Christmas without Him.

out cocoa and cookies, all the people expressed their thankfulness and shared their needs. Ed was out of work and couldn't pay his mortgage or put food on the table. Fred was new in town because he had been evicted for not paying rent and now his family was struggling. His tattered clothes showed it. Mona was well-dressed but was facing financial losses due to a bout with cancer.

As the pantry clients heard their numbers called for pickup, they noisily scrambled up the stairs to collect their groceries and holiday turkeys. I wiped down tables speckled with cookie crumbs and covered with random printed prayer requests that were left behind. Unlike at the mall, I felt joy swell up in my chest and a deep inner peace.

"'Lord, when did we see you hungry and feed you, or thirsty and give you something to drink? When did we see you a stranger and invite you in, or needing clothes and clothe you? When did we see you sick or in prison and go and visit you?' The King will reply, 'I tell you the truth, whatever you did for one of the least of these . . ., you did for me.'"
—MATTHEW 25:37–40 (NIV 1984)

After making some hefty purchases, I raced to the car and drove to the local food pantry, where I volunteered on occasion. I was greeted by a friendly deputy and a host of volunteers.

Outside was a line of two hundred families gathering for their biweekly food boxes. Extra families had shown up today because there were free turkeys for Christmas. No one was ever turned away.

As I grabbed my volunteer name tag and began walking around the fellowship hall passing

The room was empty, but my heart was full. Christmas was being marketed at the mall as a time to buy gifts, but here I found something priceless that I could not buy. Like the searching Wise Men, I had finally found evidence of the Christ Child. He was in Ed, Fred, and Mona. God whispered to my spirit, "I am in these. What you do for them, you do for Me." I had found Christ; I had found Christmas!

Christmas Eve Pageant

Louise Pugh Corder

Imagine a white frame church
perched high upon a hill
on Christmas Eve, the churchyard
snow-covered, peaceful, still.

Inside, excited small girls,
their wide eyes all alight,
are dressed as lovely angels
with halos tinsel-bright.

The playful, mischievous boys
have been transformed with grace
into wise, handsome magi
and shepherds with slow pace.

The robed young chorus enters
the cedar-draped choir loft.
Anticipation rises;
expectant hush falls soft.

A tender, quiet Mary
so humbly bows her head
before the tiny Baby
in straw-filled manger bed.

With calm assurance, Joseph
keeps watch beside the Child.
The choir sings joyous tidings of
a Savior meek and mild!

The shining star of Christmas,
through children's eyes aglow,
beams down its holy splendor
on worshipers below!

Angelus Domini nuntiavit Mariæ.

The Foretelling and Fulfilling of the Savior

Therefore the Lord himself shall give you a sign; Behold, a virgin shall conceive, and bear a son, and shall call his name Immanuel. —ISAIAH 7:14

Now the birth of Jesus Christ was on this wise: When as his mother Mary was espoused to Joseph, before they came together, she was found with child of the Holy Ghost. Then Joseph her husband, being a just man, and not willing to make her a public example, was minded to put her away privily. But while he thought on these things, behold, the angel of the Lord appeared unto him in a dream, saying, Joseph, thou son of David, fear not to take unto thee Mary thy wife: for that which is conceived in her is of the Holy Ghost. And she shall bring forth a son, and thou shalt call his name JESUS: for he shall save his people from their sins. Now all this was done, that it might be fulfilled which was spoken of the Lord by the prophet, saying, Behold, a virgin shall be with child, and shall bring forth a son, and they shall call his name Emmanuel, which being interpreted is, God with us.

Then Joseph being raised from sleep did as the angel of the Lord had bidden him, and took unto him his wife: And knew her not till she had brought forth her firstborn son: and he called his name JESUS.

—MATTHEW 1:18–25

The Savior Will Come from Bethlehem

But thou, Bethlehem Ephratah, though thou be little among the thousands of Judah,
yet out of thee shall he come forth unto me that is to be ruler in Israel;
whose goings forth have been from of old, from everlasting. —MICAH 5:2

And it came to pass in those days, that there went out a decree from Caesar Augustus, that all the world should be taxed. (And this taxing was first made when Cyrenius was governor of Syria.) And all went to be taxed, every one into his own city.

And Joseph also went up from Galilee, out of the city of Nazareth, into Judaea, unto the city of David, which is called Bethlehem; (because he was of the house and lineage of David:) To be taxed with Mary his espoused wife, being great with child.

And so it was, that, while they were there, the days were accomplished that she should be delivered. And she brought forth her firstborn son, and wrapped him in swaddling clothes, and laid him in a manger; because there was no room for them in the inn.

And there were in the same country shepherds abiding in the field, keeping watch over their flock by night. And, lo, the angel of the Lord came upon them, and the glory of the Lord shone round about them: and they were sore afraid. And the angel said unto them, Fear not: for, behold, I bring you good tidings of great joy, which shall be to all people. For unto you is born this day in the city of David a Saviour, which is Christ the Lord. And this shall be a sign unto you; Ye shall find the babe wrapped in swaddling clothes, lying in a manger. And suddenly there was with the angel a multitude of the heavenly host praising God, and saying, Glory to God in the highest, and on earth peace, good will toward men.

And it came to pass, as the angels were gone away from them into heaven, the shepherds said one to another, Let us now go even unto Bethlehem, and see this thing which is come to pass, which the Lord hath made known unto us.

And they came with haste, and found Mary, and Joseph, and the babe lying in a manger. And when they had seen it, they made known abroad the saying which was told them concerning this child. And all they that heard it wondered at those things which were told them by the shepherds.

But Mary kept all these things, and pondered them in her heart.

And the shepherds returned, glorifying and praising God for all the things that they had heard and seen, as it was told unto them.

—LUKE 2:1–20

Stained glass in Monestir Monastery of Montserrat, Barcelona, Catalonia, Spain. Photograph © Bill Perry/Shutterstock

Magi procidentes adoraverunt Eum

Kings from the East Will Worship the Savior

*The kings of Tarshish and of the isles shall bring presents: the kings of Sheba
and Seba shall offer gifts. Yea, all kings shall fall down before him:
all nations shall serve him.* —Psalm 72:10–11

Now when Jesus was born in Bethlehem of Judaea in the days of Herod the king, behold, there came wise men from the east to Jerusalem, Saying, Where is he that is born King of the Jews? for we have seen his star in the east, and are come to worship him.

When Herod the king had heard these things, he was troubled, and all Jerusalem with him. And when he had gathered all the chief priests and scribes of the people together, he demanded of them where Christ should be born. And they said unto him, In Bethlehem of Judaea: for thus it is written by the prophet, And thou Bethlehem, in the land of Juda, art not the least among the princes of Juda: for out of thee shall come a Governor, that shall rule my people Israel.

Then Herod, when he had privily called the wise men, enquired of them diligently what time the star appeared. And he sent them to Bethlehem, and said, Go and search diligently for the young child; and when ye have found him, bring me word again, that I may come and worship him also. When they had heard the king, they departed; and, lo, the star, which they saw in the east, went before them, till it came and stood over where the young child was. When they saw the star, they rejoiced with exceeding great joy.

And when they were come into the house, they saw the young child with Mary his mother, and fell down, and worshipped him: and when they had opened their treasures, they presented unto him gifts; gold, and frankincense, and myrrh.

—Matthew 2:1–11

Stained glass in Saint Peter and Paul Catholic Church of San Francisco, California. Photograph © Bill Perry/Shutterstock

NATIVITY by The Macneil Studio. Image © The Macneil Studio/Art Licensing

The Cradle: a Christmas Story

Dr. Ralph F. Wilson

They left their home, the new cradle still swinging from the rafters. Night after night the aroma of fresh-cut wood had filled the room as Joseph had patiently fashioned the tiny cradle, using the same chisel and saw he usually put down at dusk.

Now Joseph wiped the tears from Mary's cheeks and shut the door behind them. "It'll be okay," he told her, as he cinched up their belongings on the donkey.

"Joseph, can't we wait a few days? The baby could come any time." She didn't want to leave home. Not now.

"We've waited for the baby as long as we dare." He was ready to get on the road. "We have to leave today, or I'll be arrested for not appearing in Bethlehem for the census."

"At least bring the cradle, Joseph," she pleaded. "I want the baby to have something nice."

"No, it'll have to stay behind. The baby will be rocking in it soon enough."

Five days and ninety bone-weary miles later, Joseph searched the small stable where they were staying on the outskirts of crowded Bethlehem. Mary's time would be soon now. He was careful to keep his lamp from igniting the old straw. He finally settled on an ancient stone manger for the baby's bed, cut from the wall of the limestone cave that housed the animals. He reached in to scoop the last gritty bits of straw from the manger's dank bottom. "That'll have to do," he muttered. He filled the trough with an armful of fresh fodder and covered it with a folded blanket to keep the animals away.

It was well past midnight by the time Mary finished washing and wrapping her new baby. Now she lifted Him gently into His new bed. Joseph put his arm around her shoulders as they gazed at the sleeping infant.

Mary touched the tiny fingers. "That cradle you spent so much time on would be so nice right now, Joseph." She looked up at the cave's low ceiling. "You could hang it somewhere. No baby I know has a cradle like that. It's fit for a king."

Joseph grinned. "Not every boy has a carpenter for a dad," he said. But he wondered. Why couldn't little Jesus be home in that cradle? Why does this special child the angel told Mary and him about have to be born in this smelly stable? A hill-country carpenter's home is bad enough. Why here? Why Bethlehem?

The answer wasn't long in coming. An older boy poked his head in the door, startling the couple from their quiet moment. "Is there a baby in here?" he mumbled apologetically. Then he saw the tiny child. Mary picked her baby up to shield the infant from his eyes. The face disappeared.

Mary's eyes mirrored Joseph's concern. He strode to the cave's opening. He could hear a distant call, "Over here, Jake found Him!" In the darkness, Joseph could make out a handful of forms coming toward him. He gripped his stout wooden staff and stood resolutely at the door.

As they approached the stable, he could see they were shepherds. Joseph's grip on the staff tightened. The oldest one spoke hesitantly. "Can we come in? We have . . . ah . . . come to see the Christ-Child."

Joseph glanced at Mary. He could feel a tingle move down his spine. This was more than an accident. The whole fantastic course of events was far more than an accident. He nodded and stepped back into the stable. "Yes, come in. You are welcome."

The shepherds shuffled into the cramped cave. The youngest pushed in alongside the donkey to get a better view. They knelt. "God be praised!" The old shepherd spoke with deep reverence.

"It's just like the angel told us," another whispered in awe. "'Behold, I bring you good tidings of great joy, which shall be to all people,' the angel said."

"Imagine! An angel . . . talking to us!" the old man interjected with rising excitement. "And the child is right here in a stable so we can come and see Him." Rivulets of tears were inching down the shepherd's weathered face.

Joseph stared at the old man. "How did you find us?" he finally asked.

The boy who had first peeked in answered. "The angel said, 'Unto you is born this day in the city of David a Savior . . .'"

"That's here—Bethlehem—David's birthplace," the littlest boy interrupted. He thrust out his chest proudly. "King David was a shepherd, too, you know."

The older boy continued: " . . . a Savior, which is Christ the Lord."

"The Christ, the Messiah . . . He's the one!" The old man pointed to the baby.

"The angel was very specific," the young man went on. "'And this shall be a sign unto you. You shall find the babe wrapped in swaddling clothes, lying in a manger.'" He grinned. "How could we miss? We just ran into town and checked every stable until we found you . . . found Him." The boy paused. "How many newborns in Bethlehem do you know with a cattle manger for a cradle?"

Joseph chuckled. So that was it. The heavenly Father Himself had provided a bed for His child. A special cradle. A sign to these crude shepherds that God cared for them too.

Joseph squeezed Mary's hand very tightly.

There Were Shepherds

Edith Shaw Butler

The shepherds heard the angels sing
that night so long ago;
and suddenly a great light shone
and warmed them with its glow.

"Fear not, for unto you is born
in Bethlehem this day,
a Savior, which is Christ the Lord,"
they heard the angels say.

"Oh, glory in the highest now!"
the heavens seemed to ring;

"Now go ye unto Bethlehem
and see this wondrous thing."

The shepherds left their quiet flocks
to seek the stable place
and marvel at the Holy Child,
the mother's radiant face.

They did not understand the things
they heard and saw that night;
they only knew that love had filled
their hearts with hope and light.

Shepherds in the Street

Pamela Love

What's outside the window?
Do you hear the running feet?
It's the middle of the night,
and there are shepherds in the street!

They're still carrying their crooks,
and one still holds a lamb.
Where can they be going?
Are you curious? I am.

They're entering a stable.
Oh, I see a family's there.
The mother has a Newborn
Whom she treats with tender care.

The shepherds say that they came
to see that baby boy.
Though I still don't know
    what's going on,
somehow I share their joy.

Questions at Christmas

Eileen Spinelli

If I had been the
    innkeeper,
would I have made room
for a baby's bed?
Or would I have pointed,
impatient, across the dust
to a tired old shed?

If I had been a shepherd,
would I have named
the angels' song
nothing more than
wind along
the highway?

If I had been a king,
would I have left

my treasured everything
to travel far,
simply to follow
the twinkling whimsy
of a winter star?

I wasn't there that night
in Bethlehem.
And yet the questions
seem to be a part of
who I am.
Can I find room for love,
for songs of grace?
And how far would I go
to make the world
a brighter place?

Out of the east the Wise Men came;
out of the north, the south, they rise;
out of the west with hearts aflame,
the light of a star in their lifted eyes;
from heart to heart with a quickened life,
from eye to eye through the land afar,
the message flies with a whispered joy,
"He cometh! He cometh! Behold His star!"

—MARY A. LATHBURY

Long, Long Ago
Author Unknown

Winds through the olive trees
softly did blow,
round little Bethlehem
long, long ago.

Sheep on the hillside lay
whiter than snow;
shepherds were watching them,
long, long ago.

Then from the happy sky,
angels bent low,
singing their songs of joy,
long, long ago.

For in a manger bed,
cradled we know,
Christ came to Bethlehem,
long, long ago.

In Bethlehem
Mary A. Lathbury

Little town, O little town,
with a star's light falling down
like a veil of rosy light
through the soft, blue Syrian night,
what within thy walls can be
that the star has come to thee?

It has led the Eastern kings
through their long night-wanderings,
until now its glory falls
softly o'er thy still, white walls;
what hast thou to show to them,
silent little Bethlehem?

Thou hast opened now thy gate
where the kingly Wise Men wait,
and along a lowly street,
see, the star still guides their feet,
as the kings of Orient bring
gifts and worship to their King.

Who in little Bethlehem
wears the world's first diadem?
Look again; His baby brow
no sign-royal beareth now,
but—a mother's arm His throne,
earth and heaven are His own!

Bells of Peace

Pamela Kennedy

The author of this popular carol was a prodigy from an American family tracing its roots back to the Mayflower. Born in Portland, Maine, in 1807, Henry Wadsworth Longfellow entered school at the age of three and, by his sixth birthday, was reading the classics and composing poems. By nineteen, Longfellow was a professor of modern language at Bowdoin College, and by twenty-seven, he had married and been invited to join the faculty at Harvard. While on a European tour, however, tragedy struck—his wife, Mary, experienced a miscarriage and died. Brokenhearted, he buried himself in his writing.

Over seven years later, after a lengthy courtship, Longfellow married a young woman from Boston, Frances (Fanny) Appleton. In their home overlooking the Charles River, the couple often entertained such literary celebrities as Ralph Waldo Emerson, Nathaniel Hawthorne, and Julia Ward Howe. Five children filled their house with activity and laughter, and it was during this period that Henry wrote his wildly popular poems: "Evangeline," "The Song of Hiawatha," and "The Courtship of Miles Standish." He gained worldwide fame, attained financial success, and was granted honorary degrees at Oxford and Cambridge. Then tragedy struck again.

While sealing envelopes with wax, Fanny dropped a match on her skirt. Her gown caught fire, and despite Henry's attempts to extinguish the flames by smothering them with his own body, Fanny perished. Left with serious burns on his face and hands and grieving the loss of his wife, Longfellow fell into a deep depression. The onset of the Civil War only added to his sorrow. His oldest son, Charley, ran off to join the Union Army and, within a year, was wounded.

On Christmas Day, 1863, in the midst of his personal anguish, Longfellow is reported to have heard the pealing of bells. Setting pen to paper, he composed the verses of a poem titled "Christmas Bells." In its third stanza, the poem echoes the poet's despair: "'There is no peace on earth,' I said. 'For hate is strong and mocks the song of peace on earth, good will to men.'" Despite its somber tone, the poem eventually arcs to an affirmation of faith as Longfellow declares, "God is not dead, nor doth He sleep; the wrong shall fail, the right prevail, with peace on earth, good will to men."

It would be another decade before English organist John Calkin set Longfellow's poem to music, changing the title to "I Heard the Bells on Christmas Day." Today, Longfellow's legacy lives on in his only Christmas carol, reminding us that, despite our sorrows, the Christmas message still rings with hope for peace on earth, good will to men!

I Heard the Bells on Christmas Day

Henry Wadsworth Longfellow (1807–1882)   John Baptiste Calkin (1827–1905)

1. I heard the bells on Christ - mas Day their
2. I thought how, as the day had come, the
3. And in des - pair, I bow'd my head; "There
4. Then pealed the bells more loud and deep: "God

old fa - mil - iar car - ols play, and
bel - fries of all Chris - ten - dom had
is no peace on earth," I said, "for
is not dead, nor doth He sleep; the

wild and sweet the words re - peat of
roll'd a - long th' un - bro - ken song of
hate is strong and mocks the song, of
wrong shall fail, the right pre - vail with

peace on earth, good will to men.
peace on earth, good will to men.
peace on earth, good will to men."
peace on earth, good will to men."

My Christmas Wish for You

Ruth Kephart

My Christmas wish for you, my friend,
is not a simple one,
for I wish you hope and joy and peace,
days filled with warmth and sun.

I wish you love and friendship, too,
throughout the coming year,
lots of laughter and happiness
to fill your world with cheer.

May you count your blessings, one by one,
and when totaled by the lot,
may you find all you've been given
to be more than what you sought.

May your journeys be short, your burdens light;
may your spirit never grow old.
May all your clouds have silver linings
and your rainbows, pots of gold.

I wish this all and so much more—
may all your dreams come true.
May you have a Merry Christmas, friend,
and a happy New Year too.

A Christmas Wish

Grace Mathews Walker

More than a merry Christmas
I wish you this year,
more than a happy Christmas
with your loved ones dear,

more than the precious hours
with friends who are true,
more than the gifts you treasure
that others give to you—

I wish for you the blessing
of that Christmas Day
when angels sang the story
and stars marked the way.

I wish you joy unending
with much love and cheer—
I wish you peace on Christmas
and through all the year.

There'll Always Be Christmas

Edna Jaques

There'll always be Christmas . . .
as long as a light
glows in the window
to guide folks at night,
as long as a star
in the heavens above
keeps shining down,
there'll be Christmas and love.

There'll always be Christmas . . .
as long as a tree
grows on a hilltop,
as long as the sea
breaks into foam
on a white pebbled beach,
as long as there's laughter
and beautiful speech.

There'll always be Christmas . . .
as long as a street
gives back the echo
of homeward-bound feet

and children with mittens
and warm winter clothes
have bright eyes that sparkle
and cheeks like a rose.

There'll always be Christmas . . .
with holly and snow
and church bells that ring
in the valley below,
shop windows lighted
and doorways ajar
and over the housetops
the glint of a star.

The cavernous length
of a stocking to fill,
a wreath on the window,
a light on a hill,
the song of the angels,
and over again
the beautiful message—
good will among men.

Geo. Hinke

ideals

70 Years of Tradition and Inspiration

Seventy years ago, in 1944, the first issue of Ideals was published.

It was a time of sorrow and despair for many. World War II had raged on longer than anyone had imagined possible, and the war effort exacted personal and economic sacrifices from Americans at home and abroad. In the midst of such troubled times, a man with a vision of hope for a better world launched Ideals magazine.

As its founder, Van B. Hooper, noted, "Ideals is a book of old-fashioned ideals, homey philosophy, poetry, music, inspiration, and art—things some of us may have overlooked during these busy days." The first Ideals issue ran as a limited edition due to the severe paper shortage during the war. It struck an immediate chord with its readers, and readership grew quickly.

In the years since, Ideals, especially the Christmas edition, has become a tradition in homes across the country, and the issues are viewed by many as keepsakes. We trust that Ideals continues to serve as a source of hope and inspiration to you, our readers.

The pages that follow contain reproductions of classic pages from the past seven decades. As this special section illustrates, times have changed, but the timeless values and pure joys of Christmas have not.

Here are just a few of the memorable covers of past issues.

Top row, from left to right: 1944, 1946, 1952, 1961; bottom row: 1972, 1975, 1987.

At Christmastime

A. K. Rowswell

As long as there's a sun to shine
And send its light;
As long as there are stars that glow
Throughout the night;
As long as there are skies above,
And hearts that warm with throbs of love,
There will be friends we're thinking of
At Christmastime.

No matter what the days may bring
Of wealth or woe;
No matter where the paths may lead,
Through high or low;
No matter if the skies are gray,
We'll struggle on from day to day
If there be friends along the way
At Christmastime.

If we could reach across the miles
And clasp your hand;
If we could be with you today,
You'd understand;
If we could have a greeting sent
And have you know just what it meant,
We're sure your heart would be content
At Christmastime.

Song over Stables

Dana K. Akers

Under a full, white moon the farmsteads lie—
Dim shapes identified by points of light,
And here and there, smoke-plumes against the sky—
A perfect setting for this holy night.

The rooms are warm and soft with candle glow;
The ribboned gifts are placed beneath the tree,
While Christmas lore from out the long ago
Again brings near the blest Nativity.

The candles placed to guide the Holy Child;
The vision that the hillside shepherds saw
Because their hearts were meek and undefiled
And schooled in patience and humility
Are legends woven with the Christmas cheer.
And he who keeps a simple faith and strong,
As that which children know, can plainly hear
Above the fields—a shred of angel song!

Home on Christmas Day

Douglas Malloch

I bet a king upon a throne
　　　　Who looks around his court,
Whatever army he may own
　　　　Or wealth of any sort,
Is never nearly half as proud
　　　　As I was, in a way,
When I beheld our little crowd
　　　　At home on Christmas Day.

For yonder sat another queen,
　　　　As good as any king's;
You know the lady that I mean,
　　　　Who wears no royal things,
But has as faithful followers
　　　　Her wishes to obey;
God bless that retinue of hers
　　　　At home on Christmas Day!

A family of girls and boys,
　　　　Just healthy boys and girls,
No music theirs but happy noise,
　　　　No gold but golden curls.
But, Mr. King, you keep your throne!
　　　　It may be fine—but, say,
I wouldn't trade it for my own
　　　　At home on Christmas Day!

My scepter is a carving-knife,
　　　　A weapon tried and true,
My house my castle, queen my wife,
　　　　The kids our retinue.
Each wants a leg, and not a wing,
　　　　And so I carve away—
But Mother, she'll take "anything"
　　　　At home on Christmas Day.

It's over now another year,
　　　　Our Christmas Day is o'er;
But we're a little gladder here,
　　　　And closer than before.
I do not ask for riches, then—
　　　　Lord, only this I pray:
That we can have them all again
　　　　At home on Christmas Day.

The Christmas Road

Grace M. Walker

I like to think of winding roads
Where at every turning
Nature holds a glad surprise
Of gorgeous, friendly trees
And landscapes purpled
By the setting sun.

One road there is
That charms and stills
The longings of my heart
For holy, sacred things:
I see it ev'ry Christmas Eve
Stretching out o'er mountain-tops
And through the valleys deep
To a quiet little town
Wrapped in peaceful sleep.
Star-lanterns hung
On silver cords
To light the way—
And Angels sang
As man has never sung
Before or since
That Holy Night
So long ago.

The Christmas Road still beckons
And through the ages
Christmas days have come and gone
To lead mankind
Forever on to Bethlehem.
O Manger place
Wherein the tired Virgin-Mother
Sang sweet lullabies
That spoke of God's great love
For all mankind,
O humble, sacred shrine,
Forever be the safe abode
Of all who walk the Christmas Road!

Christmas Is

Garnett Ann Schultz

Christmas is a time of love,
A time of joy and cheer.
Christmas is a peaceful time,
The wondrous time of year.
A time of faith, a time of hope,
Of friendships much more true;
Christmas is a joyous time
When God shall come to you.

Christmas is a little child.
It's tinsel shining bright,
Frosted windows, snowy lanes,
Candles in the night.
It's Santa Claus and dreams come true,
So much that gladness sees;
It's holly wreaths and silver bells
And star-tipped Christmas trees.

Christmas is a place called home . . .
A door thrown open wide;
A crackling fireplace all aglow
And loving hearts inside.
It's happy faces, shining eyes,
Soft music on the air;
It's tissue, ribbons, cards to write
And secrets everywhere.

Christmas is a lighted church . . .
The very nicest part,
Believing in a special way
A prayer that fills your heart.
It's friendliness so much more real,
A blessing from above;
Christmas is the precious time
We greet the folks we love.